SIMPLE RECIPES

Essential and Revitalizing Recipes for Light Meals

Lauren Colen

work can be in any fashion deemed liable for any hardship or damages that may befall them after undertaking information described herein.

Additionally, the information in the following pages is intended only for informational purposes and should thus be thought of as universal. As befitting its nature, it is presented without assurance regarding its prolonged validity or interim quality. Trademarks that are mentioned are done without written consent and can in no way be considered an endorsement from the trademark holder.

TABLE OF CONTENTS

Introduction

During the summer season, there is nothing better than a tasty salad. The heat induces us to prefer fresh foods rich in vitamins to those that during the winter replenish our protein and caloric needs.

Salads are very versatile, healthy, and varied.

They can be enjoyed as an accompaniment to a barbecue or a menu, often even as a main meal.

Today we can divide the salads into:

- simple
- mixed
- composed

Simple salads are those prepared with only one type of vegetable; the mixed ones are prepared with different types of vegetables and both are generally considered side dishes. Compound salads can be considered unique dishes. Their composition is varied. In addition to vegetables, they can be made with foods rich in proteins (chicken, mozzarella, tuna, hard-boiled eggs, legumes, etc.) but also with fatty substances (ham, cheeses, meats, etc.).

Aside from the simple salads, the others are as tasty as they are packed with different varieties of ingredients. The uniformity and the pieces of their components ensure homogeneity of flavors and the dressing completes the harmony of the preparations.

The moment of dressing is by no means a negligible element for the taste of the salad. If seasoned long before its consumption, the vinegar or lemon and salt "cook" the leaf excessively. If, on the other hand, the dressing is done just before eating it, the taste of the salad is not harmonious and uneven. A tasty salad should be seasoned 5/6 minutes before consuming it by turning it for a long time so that the dressing is distributed evenly.

The salads are usually dressed in good quality extra virgin olive oil, salt, vinegar, or lemon. For some years now the restaurant has also been supplied with an oil and vinegar menu. The recommended oil for simple and compound salads is the delicate and slightly fruity one. For vinegar, it is important to respect the tastes of different people. Some prefer good wine vinegar, others apple vinegar, still others balsamic vinegar. It should be noted that balsamic vinegar also includes a wide range of delicious products with very different characteristics.

To ensure a homogeneous dressing for salads, it is possible to emulsify the oil, salt, lemon, or vinegar, obtaining a vinaigrette respectively. These are considered cold sauces prepared with 2/3 of oil and 1/3 of lemon or vinegar. The preparation is completed with the necessary salt and sometimes with pepper and/or mustard.

Salad Recipes

Blueberry Hemp Salad

Time required:
20 minutes

Servings: 04

INGREDIENTS	STEPS FOR COOKING

160 g fresh blueberries

4 tbsp unpeeled hemp seeds

200 g lamb's lettuce

200 g fresh mushrooms

4 tbsp lime juice

2 tbsp linseed oil

2 teaspoons of cane sugar

salt

pepper

1. Wash the lamb's lettuce thoroughly, pat dry and sort. Then wash and drain the blueberries. Then clean the mushrooms and cut into even slices.

2. Whisk 2 tbsp lime juice with the cane sugar and linseed oil and season with salt and pepper. Now fold the dressing under the lamb's lettuce.

3. Arrange the salad with the mushrooms and blueberries, top with the hemp seeds and serve.

Fruited Millet Salad

Time required:
15 minutes

Servings: 04

INGREDIENTS

1 cup millet
Zest and juice
1 orange Juice
1 lemon
3 Tbsp. brown rice
syrup
½ cup dried
unsulfured apricots,
chopped (see more
on sulfites and sulfur
dioxide)
½ cup currants
½ cup golden raisins
1 Gala apple, cored
and diced
2 Tbsp. finely
chopped mint

STEPS FOR COOKING

1. Over high heat, bring 2 quarts of lightly salted water to a boil and add the millet.

2. Return to a boil, cook for 12 to 14 minutes, reduce heat to medium, cover, and cook.

3. Drain the millet water, rinse until it is cold, and set it up.

4. Place in a large bowl the orange juice and zest, lemon juice, and brown rice syrup.

5. Whisk in order to combine.

6. Mix well and add the apricots, currants, raisins, apple, and mint. Add the cooked millet and mix to coat.

7. Before being served.

Ginger and Kohlrabi Salad

Time required:
35 minutes

Servings: 04

INGREDIENTS

10 g fresh ginger
500 g kohlrabi
2 cucumbers
300 g apple
6 tbsp walnut oil
2 teaspoons of vinegar
70 ml lemon juice
20 g fresh parsley
1 teaspoon salt

STEPS FOR COOKING

1. First, peel the fresh ginger. Then wash and peel the kohlrabi and apples. Now wash and peel the cucumber and use a spoon to scrape out the seeds. Then grate everything with a kitchen grater.

2. Drizzle the grated vegetables with the lemon juice and mix everything well.

3. Then wash the fresh parsley, pat dry and chop finely. Then mix the oil with the vinegar and whisk with salt and parsley. Now pour the dressing over the salad, mix well and let it steep for at least 15 minutes and only then serve.

Orange, Beet, and Bean Salad

Time required:
20 minutes

Servings: 04

INGREDIENTS	STEPS FOR COOKING

4 to 6 medium beets (about 1½ pounds), washed and peeled

2 oranges, zested, peeled, and segmented

2 cups cooked navy beans or one 15-ounce can, drained and rinsed

¼ cup brown rice vinegar

3 Tbsp. minced dill

Salt to taste

½ Tsp. freshly ground black pepper

4 cups mixed salad greens

1. In a saucepan, place the beets and cover them with water. Bring to a boil, cover, reduce heat and simmer until the beets are tender, or for 20 minutes. Drain and set aside to cool the beets.

2. Cut them into wedges once the beets have cooled and place them in a large bowl. Add to the beets the orange zest and segments, beans, brown rice vinegar, dill, and salt and pepper. To combine, toss lightly.

3. Divide the mixed salad greens between four individual plates in order to serve. Put the beet salad on top and garnish it with the toasted almonds, if needed.

4 Tbsp. slivered almonds, toasted, optional

Chicken Broccoli Salad with Almond Dressing

Time required:
40 minutes

Servings: 06

INGREDIENTS

2 chicken breasts
1 pound broccoli, cut into florets
1 Almond, peeled and pitted
½ lemon, juiced
2 garlic cloves
¼ teaspoon chili powder
¼ teaspoon minutes powder Salt and pepper to taste

STEPS FOR COOKING

1. Cook the chicken in a large pot of salty water.
2. Drain and cut the chicken into small cubes. Place in a salad bowl.
3. Add the broccoli and mix well.
4. Combine the Almond, lemon juice, garlic, chili powder, minutes powder, salt, and pepper in a blender. Pulse until smooth.
5. Spoon over the salad with the dressing and blend well.
6. Serve the salad fresh.

Blueberries & Spinach Salad

Time required:
15 minutes

Servings: 04

INGREDIENTS

6 cups fresh baby spinach

1½ cups fresh blueberries

¼ cup onion, sliced

¼ cup almond, sliced

¼ cup feta cheese, crumbled

For Dressing:

1/3 cup olive oil

2 tablespoons fresh lemon juice

¼ teaspoon liquid stevia

1/8 teaspoon garlic powder

Salt, as required.

STEPS FOR COOKING

1. For Salad: in a bowl, add the spinach, berries, onion and almonds and mix.

2. For Dressing: in another small bowl, add all the ingredients and beat until well blended.

3. Place the dressing over salad and gently toss to coat well.

4. Serve immediately.

Mixed Berries Salad

Time required:
20 minutes

Servings: 04

INGREDIENTS

1 cup fresh strawberries, hulled and sliced
½ cups fresh blackberries
½ cup fresh blueberries
½ cup fresh raspberries
6 cup fresh arugula
2 tablespoons extra-virgin olive oil
Salt and ground black pepper, as required

STEPS FOR COOKING

1. In a salad bowl, place all the ingredients and toss to coat well.
2. Serve immediately.

Greek Salad

Time required:
30 minutes

Servings: 02

1 large tomato,
About a quarter
peeled lettuce,
Handful of black
olives (kalamata
olives with pit are
recommended),
About a quarter of a
smaller red onion,
Feta cheese (45 g is
enough),
Olive oil (cold
pressed or "extra
virgin" is
recommended),
Small handful of
dried oregano.

1. Cut the vegetables into smaller cubes, slice the onion into thin marigolds, and mix with the olives.

2. Place feta cheese on top, drizzle with olive oil (1-2 tablespoons are enough). Grind oregano in your palms and sprinkle the salad with it.

3. Serve along with a slice of crispy pastry.

Coleslaw Salad

Time required:
19 hours

Servings: 02

INGREDIENTS

¼ small celery stalk
1 onion
1 larger carrot
1 smaller head of cabbage
Salt
Vinegar, semolina sugar, ground pepper
Mayonnaise 150 g
Whipping cream 100 ml

STEPS FOR COOKING

1. Grate cabbage into thin slices in a deep bowl. Sprinkle with salt, mix thoroughly and squeeze by hand for about 20-30 minutes so that the cabbage releases as much juice as possible and becomes brittle.

2. Next, partially drain the liquids. Roughly grate the carrots, finely chop the celery, and finely chop or grate the onions.

3. Mix everything thoroughly. Prepare the dressing by mixing sugar and mayonnaise with whipped cream.

4. Mix the ingredients for the salad, season with vinegar, pepper and salt as needed and store in the refrigerator for at least an hour.

5. Stir well again before serving. Serve real Coleslaw salad with fried, roasted

meats or just with gluten-free, low-protein bread.

Curried Rice Salad

Time required:
20 minutes

Servings: 04

INGREDIENTS

½ cup (120 g) of cooked white rice e.g., basmati

¼ small red onion, finely chopped

½ green bell pepper, diced

½ red bell pepper, diced

1 stalk of celery

1 cup of white cabbage, shredded

1 small carrot, peel and shredded

For the Dressing:

2-3 tbsp. balsamic vinegar

2-3 tbsp. of rice vinegar

2 tbsp. of mustard

STEPS FOR COOKING

1. Combine the cooked rice with the diced peppers and the rest of the vegetables.

2. In a small dressing bowl, combine the ingredients of the dressing and stir well or blend in a food processor.

3. Add the dressing to the rice and vegetable salad, toss, and serve.

INGREDIENTS	STEPS FOR COOKING
2 cloves of garlic, minced *1 tsp. of light soy sauce* *2 tsp. of curry powder*	

Salmon and Pesto Salad

Time required:
20 minutes

Servings: 02

INGREDIENTS

For the Pesto:
1 minced garlic clove
½ cup fresh arugula
¼ cup extra virgin olive oil
½ cup fresh basil
1 teaspoon black pepper
For the Salmon:
4 oz. skinless salmon fillet
1 tablespoon coconut oil
For the Salad:
½ juiced lemon
2 sliced radishes
½ cup iceberg lettuce
1 teaspoon black pepper

STEPS FOR COOKING

1. Prepare the pesto by blending all the pesto ingredients in a kitchen appliance or by grinding with a pestle and mortar. Set aside.

2. Add a skillet to the stove on medium-high heat and melt the copra oil.

3. Add the salmon to the pan.

4. Cook for 7-8 minutes and switch over.

5. Cook for an extra 3-4 minutes or until cooked through.

6. Remove fillets from the skillet and permit to rest.

7. Mix the lettuce and therefore the radishes and squeeze over the juice of ½ lemon.

8. Flake the salmon with a fork and blend through the salad.

9. Toss to coat and sprinkle with a little black pepper to serve.

Lemon Greek Salad

Time required:
30 minutes

Servings: 01

INGREDIENTS

140 oz Chicken breast
1 cup Chopped cucumber
1 cup Chopped orange/red bell pepper
1cup Wedged/sliced/chopped tomatoes
1/4 cup Chopped olives
2 tablespoons fresh parsley (finely chopped)
2 tablespoons Finely chopped red onion
5 teaspoons Lemon juice
1 teaspoon Olive oil
1 minced garlic clove

STEPS FOR COOKING

1. Preheat your grill to medium heat.
2. Grill the chicken and cook on each side until it is no longer pink or for 5 minutes.
3. Cut the chicken into tiny pieces. In your serving bowl, mix garlic, olives, and parsley. Whisk in olive oil (1 teaspoon) and lemon juice (4 teaspoons). Add onion, tomatoes, bell pepper, and cucumber.
4. Toss gently. Coat the ingredients with dressing. Add another teaspoon of lemon juice to taste. Divide the salad into two servings and put 6oz chicken on top of each salad.
5. Enjoy your meal.

Vegetable Salad with Prosciutto and Strawberries

Time required:
30 minutes

Servings: 04

INGREDIENTS

300 g Fresh strawberries
100 g Corn on the cob
1 cucumber for salad
2 tablespoons Olive oil
Juice from 1organic lemon
A few drops of balsamic vinegar, pepper
100 g Prosciutto

STEPS FOR COOKING

1. Let all washed vegetables and fruits drip. Then cut everything into smaller pieces, season with pepper, add a pinch of salt, and drizzle with oil to taste.

2. Add juice and vinegar. Finally, add a piece of prosciutto to each plate (about 30 g per serving).

3. Prosciutto can be substituted with chicken or beef. It is only necessary to follow the recommended amount.

4. You can add toasted points from low-protein or gluten-free pastries to the salad.

Chicken & Orange Salad

Time required:
30 minutes

Servings: 04

INGREDIENTS

For Chicken:
4 (6-ounce)
boneless, skinless
chicken breast
halves
Salt and ground
black pepper, as
required
2 tablespoons extra-
virgin olive oil
For Salad:
8 cups fresh baby
arugula
5 medium oranges,
peeled and
sectioned 1 cup
onion, sliced
For Dressing:
2 tablespoons extra-
virgin olive oil

STEPS FOR COOKING

1. For chicken: season each chicken breast half with salt and black pepper evenly.

2. Place chicken over a rack set in a rimmed baking sheet.

3. Refrigerate for at least 30 minutes.

4. Remove the baking sheet from refrigerator and pat dry the chicken breast halves with paper towels.

5. Heat the oil in a 12-inch sauté pan over medium-low heat.

6. Place the chicken breast halves, smooth-side down, and cook for about 9-10 minutes, without moving.

7. Flip the chicken breasts and cook for about 6 minutes or until cooked through.

INGREDIENTS

2 tablespoons fresh orange juice
2 tablespoons balsamic vinegar
1½ teaspoons shallots, minced
1 garlic clove, minced
Salt and ground black pepper, as required

STEPS FOR COOKING

8. Remove the sauté pan from heat and let the chicken stand in the pan for about 3 minutes.

9. Transfer the chicken breasts onto a cutting board for about 5 minutes.

10. Cut each chicken breast half into desired-sized slices.

11. For Salad: place all ingredients in a salad bowl and mix.

12. Add chicken slices and stir to combine.

13. For Dressing: place all ingredients in another bowl and beat until well combined.

14. Place the salad onto each serving plate.

15. Drizzle with dressing and serve.

Summer Cobb Salad

Time required:
30 minutes

Servings: 06

INGREDIENTS

*2 large boneless,
skinless chicken
breasts*
*1 tablespoon olive
oil*
Salt and pepper
*2 romaine hearts,
chopped*
*3 hardboiled eggs,
peeled and chopped*
*2/3 cup crumbled
blue cheese*
*2 avocados,
chopped*
1 cup blackberries
1 cup raspberries
*1 cup toasted
almonds*
*Creamy Garlic Lime
Dressing Recipe*

STEPS FOR COOKING

1. Preheat the grill. Then rub the chicken breasts with oil, and salt, and pepper liberally. Grill for 5 minutes per side over medium heat. Allow the chicken to rest for at least 5 minutes before chopping. Then cut into bite-sized pieces.

2. Meanwhile chop the romaine lettuce, eggs, and avocados. Place the lettuce on a large serving platter or bowl.

3. Arrange all the toppings over the bed of lettuce and serve with Creamy Garlic Lime Vinaigrette.

Lettuce Hot Dogs

Time required:
30 minutes

Servings: 04

INGREDIENTS

4 big lettuce leaves
4 low-sodium
frankfurter sausages
1 small onion,
chopped
1 slice of bacon, cut
into bits Drizzle of
mustard

STEPS FOR COOKING

1. Cook the sausages on the grill for 2-3 minutes on each side.
2. While the frankfurters are cooked, sauté the bacon bits in a small pan until nice and crisp.
3. Assemble each hot dog by layering one dog on each lettuce leaf, and adding the onion, bacon bits on top. Drizzle with mustard to finish.
4. Serve while hot.

Arlecchino Rice Salad

Time required:
25 minutes

Servings: 03

INGREDIENTS	STEPS FOR COOKING

INGREDIENTS

½ cup white rice, dried

1 cup chicken stock

1 zucchini, shredded

2 tablespoons capers

1 carrot, shredded

1 tomato, chopped

1 tablespoon apple cider vinegar

½ teaspoon salt

2 tablespoons fresh parsley, chopped

1 tablespoon canola oil

STEPS FOR COOKING

1. Put rice in the pan.
2. Add chicken stock and boil it with the closed lid for 15-20 minutes or until rice absorbs all water.
3. Meanwhile, in the mixing bowl combine together shredded zucchini, capers, carrot, and tomato.
4. Add fresh parsley.
5. Make the dressing: mix up together canola oil, salt, and apple cider vinegar.
6. Chill the cooked rice little and add it in the salad bowl to the vegetables.
7. Add dressing and mix up salad well.

Colorful Bean Salad

Time required:
11 minutes

Servings: 04

INGREDIENTS

200 g green beans
1 onion
1 bell pepper
1 small can (drained weight 250 g) white beans
1 small can (drained weight 250 g) kidney beans
2 tbsp wine vinegar
2 tbsp sour cream
1/2 teaspoon mustard
1/2 teaspoon tomato ketchup
1/2 teaspoon horseradish salt pepper
1 tbsp oil chopped thyme

STEPS FOR COOKING

8. Clean and wash the green beans and cook in salted boiling water for 6-8 minutes until they are firm to the bite. Pour into a sieve, rinse in cold water and drain well. Transfer to a large bowl.

9. Skin the onion and cut into thin rings. Halve and core the peppers lengthways, wash and cut into cubes. Drain the kidney beans and white beans each into a sieve, rinse with cold water and drain well. Then add the onion, bell pepper, kidney beans, and white beans to the green beans.

10. For the dressing mix together vinegar, sour cream, mustard, tomato ketchup, horseradish, oil, and thyme, season with salt and pepper. Mix with the salad ingredients and let the bean

INGREDIENTS	STEPS FOR COOKING
	salad steep for about 5 minutes before serving.

Israeli Pasta Salad

Time required:
15 minutes

Servings: 02

INGREDIENTS

2 bell peppers, chopped

3 oz. Feta cheese, chopped

1 red onion, chopped

1 tomato, chopped

1 cucumber, chopped

½ cup elbow macaroni, dried

1 teaspoon dried oregano

1 tablespoon lemon juice

1 teaspoon olive oil

1 cup water for macaroni

STEPS FOR COOKING

1. Pour water in the pan, add macaroni and boil them according to the

2. Directions of the manufacturer (approx. 15 minutes).

3. Then drain water and chill the macaroni a little.

4. Meanwhile, in the salad bowl, mix up together Feta cheese, bell peppers, onion, tomato, and cucumber.

5. Make the dressing for the salad: combine dried oregano, lemon juice, and olive oil.

6. Add cooked macaroni to the salad bowl and mix up well.

7. Drizzle the salad with dressing and shake gently.

Potato Carrot Salad

Time required:
25 minutes

Servings: 01

INGREDIENTS

Water
1 potato, sliced into cubes
1/2 carrots, cut into cubes
1/6 tablespoon milk
1/6 tablespoon Dijon mustard
1/24 cup mayonnaise
Pepper to taste
1/3 teaspoons fresh thyme, chopped
1/6 stalk celery, chopped
1/6 scallions, chopped
1/6 slice turkey bacon, cooked crispy and crumbled

STEPS FOR COOKING

1. Fill your pot with water.
2. Place it over medium-high heat.
3. Boil the potatoes and carrots for 10 to 12 minutes or until tender.
4. Drain and let cool.
5. In a bowl, mix the milk, mustard, mayonnaise, pepper, and thyme.
6. Stir in the potatoes, carrots, and celery.
7. Coat evenly with the sauce.
8. Cover and refrigerate for 4 hours.
9. Top with the scallions and turkey bacon bits before serving.

Vegetable Salad with Rice Noodles

Time required:
20 minutes

Servings: 04

*200 g Rice noodles
Seeded cucumber
and sliced
cucumber.
200 g Cherry halved
tomatoes
Handful of fresh
mint leaves
Handful of fresh
coriander leaves
Handful of chopped
iceberg lettuce
80 ml Quality fish
sauce
Lime juice 3
Sliced lemon grass
½ pieces.Finely
chopped chili
peppers,*

STEPS FOR COOKING

1. Place the cooked rice noodles in a bowl and add the tomatoes, mint, lettuce, coriander, and cucumber.

2. Next, prepare a dressing, whisking the sauce, lime juice, sugar, lemon. grass, chili pepper.

3. Pour the finished dressing over the salad and mix. You may wish to add 30 g of dry unsalted, roasted peanuts chopped. Doing this will increase the energy value of the salad.

Eggplant Salad

Time required:
30 minutes

Servings: 03

INGREDIENTS

2 eggplants, peeled and sliced
2 garlic cloves
2 green bell paper, sliced, seeds removed
½ cup fresh parsley
½ cup egg-free mayonnaise
Salt and black pepper

STEPS FOR COOKING

1. Preheat your oven to 480°F.
2. Take a baking pan and add the eggplants and black pepper.
3. Bake for about 30 minutes.
4. Flip the vegetables after 20 minutes.
5. Then take a bowl and add the baked vegetables and all the remaining ingredients.
6. Mix well.
7. Serve and enjoy!

Tuna Salad with Cranberries

Time required:
10 minutes

Servings: 04

INGREDIENTS	STEPS FOR COOKING
2 (5 ounce) cans solid white tuna packed in water, drained *2 tablespoons mayonnaise* *1/3 teaspoon dried dill weed* *3tablespoons dried cranberries*	1. Place the tuna in a bowl, and mash with a fork. 2. Mix in mayonnaise to evenly coat tuna. Mix in dill and cranberries.

Sun-Dried Tomato Chicken Pasta Salad

Time required:
20 minutes

Servings: 04

INGREDIENTS

1 pound small dried pasta (any variety)

2 cups chopped leftover cooked chicken or rotisserie chicken

1 cup fresh baby spinach, packed

7 ounces sun-dried tomatoes in oil, drained

5 ounces pitted green olives, halved

1/3 cup chopped red onion

3/4 cup light mayonnaise

1/4 cup red wine vinegar

1 tablespoon dried Italian seasoning

STEPS FOR COOKING

1. Place a large pot of salted water on the stovetop and bring to a boil. Cook the pasta according to package instructions. Drain the pasta in a colander and rinse with cold water to cool. Allow the paste to drain while you prep the remaining ingredients.

2. Chop the sun-dried tomatoes into bite-sized pieces. Place the mayonnaise, red wine vinegar, Italian seasoning, garlic, crushed red pepper, and 1/4 cup chopped sun-dried tomatoes in the blender jar. Cover and puree.

3. Place the cooled pasta, chopped chicken, spinach, remaining chopped sun-dried tomatoes, olives, and onions in a large salad bowl. Add the creamy dressing and toss to coat.

INGREDIENTS

1 clove garlic, peeled
1/4 teaspoon
crushed red pepper

STEPS FOR COOKING

Cover the bowl with plastic wrap and refrigerate until ready to serve.

Panzanella Salad

Time required:
15 minutes

Servings: 04

INGREDIENTS

2 cucumbers, chopped

1 red onion, sliced

2 red bell peppers, chopped

¼ cup fresh cilantro, chopped

1 tablespoon capers

1 oz whole-grain bread, chopped

1 tablespoon canola oil

½ teaspoon minced garlic

1 tablespoon Dijon mustard

1 teaspoon olive oil

1 teaspoon lime juice

STEPS FOR COOKING

1. Pour canola oil into the skillet and bring it to boil.

2. Add chopped bread and roast it until crunchy (3-5 minutes).

3. Meanwhile, in the salad bowl, combine sliced red onion, cucumbers, bell peppers, cilantro, capers, and mix up gently.

4. Make the dressing: mix up together lime juice, olive oil, Dijon mustard, and minced garlic.

5. Transfer the dressing over the salad and stir it directly before serving.

Buffalo Chicken Lettuce Wraps

Time required:
20 minutes

Servings: 04

INGREDIENTS

For the Buffalo Chicken Filling:
1 lb., Chicken tenderloin –cut into 1/2-inch cubes
3 tablespoons Vegetable oil
2/3 cup Crumbled blue cheese
¼ cup.Light blue cheese dressing
¼ cup Sour cream
Hot pepper sauce
2 stalks, Finely chopped celery trimmed
2 Tablespoons Chopped fresh cilantro

STEPS FOR COOKING

1. To make the buffalo chicken filling:
2. In a bowl, combine the chicken, celery, hot pepper sauce, blue cheese, and sour cream.
3. Mix the ingredients with a spoon until well combined.
4. Cover the bowl and store in the refrigerator until ready to use. To make the lettuce wraps:
5. Place the lettuce leaves on a platter or plate.
6. Divide the chicken mixture over the leaves and garnish with the celery sticks.
7. Serve the lettuce wraps cold or at room temperature.

INGREDIENTS

STEPS FOR COOKING

For the Lettuce Wraps:
8 Butter head lettuce leaves
4 Celery sticks cut into smaller pieces

Beet Feta Salad

Time required:
40 minutes

Servings: 04

INGREDIENTS

4 cups baby salad greens
½ sweet onion, sliced
8 small beets, trimmed
2 tablespoons + 1 teaspoon extra-virgin olive oil
1 tablespoon white wine vinegar
1 teaspoon Dijon mustard Black pepper (ground), to taste
2 tablespoons crumbled feta cheese 2 tablespoons walnut pieces

STEPS FOR COOKING

1. Preheat an oven to 400 ⁰ F. Grease an aluminum foil with some cooking spray.
2. Add beets with 1 teaspoon of olive oil; combine and wrap foil.
3. Bake for 30 minutes until it becomes tender. Cut beets into wedges.
4. In a mixing bowl, add remaining olive oil, vinegar, black pepper, and mustard. Combine to mix well with each other.
5. In a mixing bowl, add salad greens, onion, feta cheese, and walnuts. Combine to mix well with each other.
6. Add half of the prepared vinaigrette and toss well.
7. Add beet and combine well.
8. Drizzle remaining vinaigrette and serve fresh.

INGREDIENTS	STEPS FOR COOKING

9. Preheat the oven to 425°F or 205°C. Mix the egg and water to make the egg wash and apply the egg white over it.

10. Finally, make a clear cut on the top and bake it for 18 to 20 minutes. Lower the heat to 350°F or 175°C and bake for 10 more minutes.

11. Once done, take it out of the oven and allow it to cool.

12. Serve and enjoy.

Chicken Caesar Pasta Salad

Time required:
35 minutes

Servings: 04

INGREDIENTS	STEPS FOR COOKING

INGREDIENTS

1 1/2 pounds boneless skinless chicken breasts

1 pound fusilli pasta

1-pint grape tomatoes

1 cup pitted black olives

1 cup chopped green onions

1 head romaine lettuce

3/4 cup shredded Parmesan cheese

2 cups croutons, store-bought or homemade

STEPS FOR COOKING

1. Preheat the grill to medium heat. Place a large pot of salted water over high heat and bring to a boil. Salt and pepper the chicken breasts.

2. Once the grill is hot, grill the chicken for 5-6 minutes per side. Then remove from heat and allow it to rest. Meanwhile, drop the pasta in the boiling water. Cook for 6-8 minutes, then drain and cool.

3. Place all the ingredients for the homemade Caesar dressing in the blender. Puree until smooth. Chop the chicken breasts into bite-size pieces and roughly chop the romaine lettuce.

4. To assemble, place the pasta, tomatoes, black olives, and chopped green onions in a large bowl. Top with the chopped grilled chicken Then pour

Homemade Caesar
Dressing

Salt and pepper

For The Homemade
Caesar Dressing:

1 cup low-fat
buttermilk

1/2 cup light
mayonnaise

1 1/2 tablespoons
lemon juice

1 tablespoon Dijon
mustard

7 whole anchovies
from a can

2 cloves garlic,
peeled

the dressing over the pasta salad and toss to coat. If making ahead, cover the Chicken Caesar Pasta Salad and refrigerate until ready to serve.

5. Right before serving, toss in the chopped romaine, shredded Parmesan cheese, and croutons. Salt and pepper to taste. Serve cold or at room temperature.

Tofu & Quinoa Salad

Time required:
40 minutes

Servings: 04

INGREDIENTS	STEPS FOR COOKING

12 oz. (336g) extra firm tofu, pat dried and cut into small cubes
1 big Boston lettuce head, roughly chopped
½ cup (125g) cooked quinoa
½ cup (112ml) olive oil
1 tbsp. mustard
1 tsp. honey
Salt-pepper

1. Place water, molasses, yeast, wheat flour, ground flaxseed, oat bran, bread flour, amaranth seeds, salt, and rolled oats in the pan of a bread machine in the order suggested by the manufacturer.
2. Select the dough cycle; press start and allow the device to run the complete dough cycle.
3. Turn dough onto a lightly floured surface. Form dough into two loaves and place on a baking stone.
4. Cover the bread with a dampened cloth and let rise until the volume doubles, about 1 hour.
5. Preheat oven to 375 degrees F.
6. Bake in the preheated oven until the top is golden brown, 20 to 25 minutes. Slide the loaf onto a work surface and

INGREDIENTS	STEPS FOR COOKING
	gently tap the bottom of the loaf. If it sounds hollow, bread is done.

Chicory Puck Salad

Time required:
10 minutes

Servings: 04

INGREDIENTS	STEPS FOR COOKING

INGREDIENTS

65 g Chicory buds
40 g Apple
25 g Orange
Lemon juice
5 g Sugar
Salt

STEPS FOR COOKING

1. Clean the chicory buds, cut them into fine strips, and let stand.
2. Drain the infused bitter juice. Peel an apple and cut it into cubes.
3. Peel an orange and peel the flesh, which are then cut into small pieces. Mix chicory buds with cubes of apples and oranges.
4. Drizzle the salad with lemon juice, lightly salt, season with sugar, and mix well.

Prosciutto Salad

Time required:
10 minutes

Servings: 04

INGREDIENTS

7 oz. prosciutto

2 cups arugula

1 cup cherry tomatoes

2 cucumbers

1 tablespoon mustard

1tablespoon canola oil

¼ teaspoon dried oregano

¼ teaspoon dried dill

¼ teaspoon dried basil

1 tablespoon lemon juice

STEPS FOR COOKING

1. Chop prosciutto roughly and place in the salad bowl.
2. Then tear the arugula and add to the salad bowl too.
3. Cut cherry tomatoes into halves and chop cucumbers.
4. Add the vegetables to the salad bowl.
5. Shake the vegetable mixture well.
6. Make the dressing: whisk together mustard, canola oil, dried oregano, dill, basil, and lemon juice.
7. Pour the dressing over the salad.
8. Stir the salad gently directly before serving.

Chicken and Quinoa Salad with Pomegranate

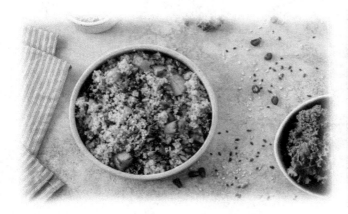

Time required:
30 minutes

Servings: 03

INGREDIENTS

½ cup quinoa

1 cup chicken stock

½ teaspoon salt

1 oz. pomegranate seeds

8 oz. chicken breast, skinless, boneless

1 tablespoon olive oil

1 cup lettuce, chopped

½ teaspoon paprika

½ teaspoon ground black pepper

1 teaspoon lemon juice

One teaspoon butter

STEPS FOR COOKING

1. In the pan, combine quinoa and chicken stock.

2. Add salt and boil the ingredients for 15 minutes or until quinoa will absorb all liquid.

3. Meanwhile, chop the chicken breast and sprinkle it with paprika and ground black pepper.

4. Place it in the skillet, add butter, and roast for 10 minutes. Stir the chicken from time to time.

5. When the chicken and quinoa are cooked, chill them to room temperature and put in the salad bowl.

6. Add pomegranate seeds, lettuce, olive oil, and lemon juice.

7. Mix up the salad well.

Vietnamese Cold Chicken Salad (Goi Ga)

Time required:
20 minutes

Servings: 08

INGREDIENTS

For The Vietnamese Cold Chicken Salad:

6 cups shredded napa cabbage

2 1/2 cups cooked shredded chicken, cold (use leftovers or a rotisserie chicken)

3/4 cup fresh mint, roughly chopped

3/4 cup shredded carrots

1/2 red onion, peeled and sliced thin

1/2 cup fresh cilantro, roughly chopped

STEPS FOR COOKING

1. Place all the salad ingredients in a large bowl.

2. In a small bowl, whisk together the lime juice, water, honey, fish sauce, and chili garlic sauce.

3. When ready to serve, pour the dressing over the salad and toss well.

1/2 cup chopped roasted peanuts (cashews for paleo-friendly)

For The Nuoc Cham Dressing:

1/4 cup fresh lime juice

1/4 cup water

3tablespoons honey

2 tablespoons fish sauce

1 teaspoon chili garlic sauce

Kale, Apple & Goat Cheese Salad

Time required:
15 minutes

Servings: 02

INGREDIENTS

1 enormous bunch of kale

1 medium green apple, sliced

2 oz. (55g) of goat cheese, crumbled

1 tbsp. white bread croutons

2 tbsp. of Dijon mustard

1 tbsp. of olive oil

1 tbsp. of lemon

1 tsp. Of honey

½ tsp. thyme

Salt/Pepper

STEPS FOR COOKING

1. Cut the kale into big and rough parts (with your hands or with a knife).

2. Add the slices of the apple and the goat cheese and toss everything together.

3. In a small bowl or food processor, mix the olive oil, lemon, mustard, honey, thyme, salt, and pepper until smooth.

4. Pour the dressing over the salad and toss well. Add the croutons on top and lightly toss again. Serve.

Chicken Apple Crunch Salad

Time required:
30 minutes

Servings: 04

INGREDIENTS	STEPS FOR COOKING

2 cups of cooked chicken
1 cup of Gala apple
½ cup of celery
1 tablespoon of scallions
¼ cup of dark raisins
1/3 cup of low-fat mayonnaise
1 tablespoon of low-fat sour cream
1 teaspoon of lemon juice
¼ teaspoon of cinnamon
¼ teaspoon of black pepper

1. Cube the cooked chicken, dice the apple and celery, and chop the scallions
2. Use a large salad bowl to combine and mix the chicken, apple, celery, scallions, and raisins
3. Whisk together the mayonnaise, lemon juice, sour cream, cinnamon, and black pepper. Pour on top of the chicken apple mixture and toss
4. Store in the refrigerator to chill before serving

Fruited Curry Chicken Salad

Time required:
45 minutes

Servings: 08

INGREDIENTS

Four cooked skinless and boneless chicken breasts

1 stalk of celery

½ cup of onion

1 medium-sized apple

¼ cup of seedless red grapes

¼ cup of seedless green grapes

½ cup of canned water chestnuts

1/3 teaspoon of black pepper

½ teaspoon of curry powder

¾ cup of mayonnaise

STEPS FOR COOKING

1. Dice the chicken and chop the celery, onion, and apple. Also, drain and chop the water chestnuts

2. Combine and mix the chicken, celery, apple, grapes, onion, water chestnuts, pepper, curry powder, and mayonnaise in a large bowl.

3. Toss all ingredients together, then serve or chill.

Shrimp Salad

Time required:
20 minutes

Servings: 02

INGREDIENTS

2 tablespoons olive oil

1/3 cup red onion, chopped

3 cups broccoli slaw

3 cups broccoli florets

1/2 teaspoon salt

2 garlic cloves, minced

1/2 pound shrimp, peeled and deveined

1 teaspoon lime juice

Green onions, chopped, for garnish

Cilantro, chopped

Sriracha and red pepper flakes, for garnish

STEPS FOR COOKING

1. Mix all the sesame almond dressing in a bowl.

2. Saute onion with oil in a skillet for 5 minutes.

3. Stir in broccoli slaw and florest then saute for 7 minutes.

4. Add black pepper and salt then transfer to a plate.

5. Add minced garlic, shrimp, lime juice and more oil to the same skillet.

6. Saute for 5 minutes then transfer the shrimp to the broccoli.

7. Pour the sesame dressing on top and garnish with cilantro and green onions.

8. Serve warm.

1 tbsp water

1 tbsp turbinado
sugar, if desired

*Sesame Almond
Dressing:*

2 tablespoons
almond butter

2 tablespoons water

1 tablespoon
sesame oil

1 tablespoon tamari

1 tablespoon maple
syrup

1 teaspoon lime
juice

1 teaspoon ginger,
minced

1 clove minced garlic

1 teaspoon sriracha
sauce

1/4 teaspoon black
pepperNutella
spread, optional for
serving

Jamaica Salad

Time required:
5 minutes

Servings: 02

INGREDIENTS	STEPS FOR COOKING

25 g Lettuce

25 g Orange

25 g Pineapple

25 g Kiwi

50 ml Orange juice (100%)

Salt

1. Wash the lettuce well and cut it into smaller pieces.
2. Remove the skin, kiwi, and pineapple from the skins and inedible parts and cut into small cubes.
3. Mix ingredients together and pour over slightly salted orange juice.

Turkey Waldorf Salad

Time required:
30 minutes

Servings: 04

INGREDIENTS

12 ounces of unsalted and cooked turkey breast

3 medium-sized red apples

1 cup of celery

½ cup of onion

¼ cup of mayonnaise

1 tablespoon of apple juice

STEPS FOR COOKING

1. Cut the turkey into cubes, dice the celery and apples and chop the onion

2. Combine and mix the turkey, apple, celery, and onion in a medium-sized bowl

3. Add the mayonnaise and apple juice, stir until it is well mixed

4. Chill in the refrigerate until ready to serve

5. Preheat the oven to 350°F or 175°C. Mix the egg and water to make the egg wash and apply the egg white over the rolls.

6. Finally, bake for 23 to 25 minutes or until golden in color.

7. Once done, take them out of the oven and allow them to cool.

8. Serve and enjoy.

Cabbage and Pear Salad

Time required:
1 hour

Servings: 06

INGREDIENTS

2 scallions, chopped

2 cups finely shredded green cabbage

1 cup finely shredded red cabbage

½ red bell pepper, boiled and chopped

½ cup chopped cilantro

2 celery stalks, chopped

1 Asian pear, cored and grated

¼ cup olive oil Juice of 1 lime Zest of 1 lime

1 teaspoon granulated sugar

STEPS FOR COOKING

1. In a mixing bowl, add cabbages, scallions, celery, pear, red pepper, and cilantro. Combine to mix well with each other.

2. Take another mixing bowl; add olive oil, lime juice, lime zest, and sugar. Combine to mix well with each other.

3. Add dressing over and toss well.

4. Refrigerate for 1 hour; serve chilled.

Japanese Ginger Salad Dressing

Time required:
10 minutes

Servings: 08

INGREDIENTS

1 cup carrots roughly chopped

½ cup onion peeled and roughly chopped

¼ cup celery roughly chopped

½ cup rice vinegar

1/3 cup canola oil

3 tablespoons fresh grated ginger

2 tablespoons granulated sugar or honey

1-2 tablespoons soy sauce (I always buy GF and low sodium.)

1 small garlic clove

STEPS FOR COOKING

1. Roughly chop all the produce. Place in the blender.

2. Add all other ingredients to the blender. If you are sensitive to sodium, start with 1 tablespoon of soy sauce. You can always add more if needed.

3. Cover the blender and turn on high. Puree until smooth. Taste, then add more soy sauce if desired.

4. Refrigerate until ready to serve.

Taco Mason Jar Salad

Time required:
25 minutes

Servings: 02

INGREDIENTS

Beef:

½ pound (227 g) 90 to 94% lean ground beef

½ tablespoon taco seasoning

Dressing:

½ cup loosely packed fresh cilantro

⅓ cup nonfat plain Greek yogurt Juice of half a lime

1 clove garlic Pinch salt Salad:

½ cup Pico de Gallo (see below)

½ cup reduced-fat Mexican blend shredded cheese

STEPS FOR COOKING

1. Make the Pico de Gallo
2. Mix together the tomato, onion, pepper, cilantro, lime juice, and salt in a bowl. Stir well with a fork to incorporate. Set aside.
3. Make the Salad
4. Heat a medium skillet over medium-high heat. Add the beef and sprinkle with the taco seasoning, and cook until the beef is browned, stirring occasionally.
5. Meanwhile, combine the cilantro, yogurt, lime juice, garlic, and salt in a blender and purée until smooth.
6. Assemble the mason jar salads: Evenly divide each salad ingredient among two mason jars and layer in the following order: dressing, pico de gallo, beef, cheese, bell pepper, and

1 medium-sized bell pepper, diced

3 cups shredded lettuce

Pico de Gallo:

1 tomato, diced

½ large white onion, diced

½ jalapeño pepper, stemmed, seeded, and diced

2 tablespoons chopped fresh cilantro

1 tablespoon freshly squeezed lime juice

⅛ teaspoon salt

shredded lettuce. Cover and refrigerate until ready to eat.

Banana and Apple Pudding Salad

Time required:
5 minutes

Servings: 04

INGREDIENTS

2 medium firm bananas, peeled and sliced

Pudding:

1 medium green apple, cored and chopped

1 (11 oz) can mandarin oranges, drained

1 (15 oz) can peach slices, drained

1 (20 oz) can pineapple tidbits, drained

1 (3.4 oz) package instant vanilla pudding

¾ cup sour cream

1 ½ cups milk

STEPS FOR COOKING

1. Mix all salad ingredients in a bowl.
2. Add pudding ingredients to a bowl and mix smoothly. Pour pudding over salad and mix well.
3. Serve immediately.

INGREDIENTS	STEPS FOR COOKING
1/3 cup orange juice2 tbsp poppy seeds	

Dutchess Peach Salad

Time required:
20 minutes

Servings: 01

INGREDIENTS

1/2 C. orange marmalade

1 (11 oz.) cans mandarin orange segments, drained reserving syrup

1/2 tsp almond extract

3 kiwi fruits, peeled and sliced

2 small peaches, sliced

1/2 pint strawberry, halved

1 C. red seedless grapes

1 C. cantaloupe, chunks

1 C. honeydew melon, chunks

STEPS FOR COOKING

1. In a bowl, add the reserved orange syrup, marmalade and almond extract and mix until well combined.

2. In a glass bowl, place the orange segments, kiwi, peaches, strawberries, grapes and melon chunks according to your desired pattern.

3. Place the marmalade mixture on top evenly.

4. With a plastic wrap, cover the bowl and place in the fridge for about 1 hour.

5. Enjoy.

Melon, Tomato & Onion Salad with Goat Cheese

Time required:
30 minutes

Servings: 08

INGREDIENTS

1 cup very thinly sliced sweet white onion, separated into rings

1 small firm-ripe melon

2 large tomatoes, very thinly sliced

1 small cucumber, very thinly sliced

½ teaspoon kosher salt

¼ teaspoon freshly ground pepper

1 cup crumbled goat cheese

¼ cup extra-virgin olive oil

STEPS FOR COOKING

1. Place onion rings in a medium bowl, add cold water to cover and a handful of ice cubes. Set aside for about 20 minutes. Drain and pat dry.

2. Meanwhile, cut melon in half lengthwise and scoop out the seeds.

3. Remove the rind with a sharp knife. Place each melon half cut-side down and slice crosswise into 1/8-inch-thick slices.

4. Make the salad on a large platter or 8 individual salad plates. Begin by arranging a ring of melon slices around the edge. Top with a layer of overlapping tomato slices. Arrange a second ring of melon slices toward the center. Top with the remaining tomato slices. Tuck cucumber slices

4 teaspoons balsamic vinegar
⅓ cup very thinly sliced fresh basil

between the layers of tomato and melon. Sprinkle with salt and pepper. Top with goat cheese and the onion rings. Drizzle with oil and vinegar. Sprinkle with basil.

Lean, Green Buddha Bowl

Time required:
1 hours

Servings: 04

INGREDIENTS

2 lbs chicken breast
¼ cup pompeian organic extra virgin olive oil
2 tablespoons lemon juice
3 cloves garlic, minced
1 tablespoon olive oil
1 lb brussels sprouts, trimmed and halved
Salt and pepper
2 cups cooked quinoa
1 cup chopped red apple, such as honeycrisp
¼ cup pepitas

STEPS FOR COOKING

1. In a zip-top bag combine chicken breasts, olive oil, lemon juice, and garlic. Allow chicken to marinate for 1 hour.

2. Preheat an outdoor grill to medium heat. Add chicken breasts to the hot grill. Cook chicken for 5-6 minutes per side.

3. Place an iron skillet on your outdoor grill. Fill the skillet with oil add brussels sprouts. The sprouts should take about minutes per side. Sprinkle with salt and pepper. When slightly soft and charred remove the skillet from the grill.

4. In a bowl, whisk together the mayo, yogurt, mustard, and vinegar. Stir in salt, fresh basil, and garlic.

INGREDIENTS

1 avocado, sliced
1 ½ cups arugula
½ cup of mayo
¾ cup plain greek yogurt
1 teaspoon stone-ground mustard
¼ cup pompeian white balsamic vinegar
½ teaspoon salt
1 tablespoon chopped fresh basil
1 clove of minced garlic

STEPS FOR COOKING

5. Divide quinoa between 4 bowls. Divide the avocado, arugula, cooked brussels sprouts, pepitas, and apples between each bowl. Dollop each green goddess dressing.

Fresh Green Grape Salad

Time required:
15 minutes

Servings: 08

INGREDIENTS

4 pounds seedless green grapes

8 ounce cream cheese

8 ounce sour cream

1/2 cup white sugar

1 teaspoon vanilla extract

4 ounces pecans – chopped

2 tablespoons brown sugar

STEPS FOR COOKING

1. First, rinse and dry the grapes.
2. Combine the vanilla, sugar, sour cream, and cream cheese into the bowl.
3. Add grapes and combine well incorporated.
4. Sprinkle with pecans and brown sugar and combine again.
5. Heat oven at a heating capacity of 375°F. Fill up the fat. Bake for 25 minutes in a 375°F furnace or until top is browned and when tapped the loaf sounds hollow. Switch the bread onto the wire rack from the pan. Let's have fun.

Shrimp and Greens Salad

Time required:
15 minutes

Servings: 06

INGREDIENTS

3 tablespoons olive oil, divided

1 garlic clove, crushed and divided

2 tablespoons fresh rosemary, chopped

1 pound (454 g) shrimp, peeled and deveined

Salt and ground black pepper, to taste

4 cups fresh arugula

2 cups lettuce, torn

2 tablespoons fresh lime juice

STEPS FOR COOKING

1. In a large wok, heat 1 tablespoon of oil over medium heat and sauté 1 garlic clove for about 1 minute.

2. Add the shrimp with salt and black pepper and cook for about 4 to 5 minutes.

3. Remove from the heat and set aside to cool.

4. Ina large bowl, add the shrimp, arugula, remaining oil, lime juice, salt and black pepper and gently, toss to coat.

5. Serve immediately.

Macaroni Salad

Time required:
10 minutes

Servings: 04

INGREDIENTS	STEPS FOR COOKING

¼ tsp. celery seed
2 hard-boiled eggs
2 cups salad dressing
1 onion
2 tsp. white vinegar
2 stalks celery
2 cups cooked macaroni
1 red bell pepper
2 tbsps. mustard

1. In a bowl, add all ingredients and mix well
2. Serve with dressing.

Tabbouleh Salad

Time required:
2 hours

Servings: 08

INGREDIENTS

½ cup of dry bulgur

1 medium-sized tomato

1 medium-sized cucumber

1bunch of green onions

2 bunches of parsley

½ bunch of mint

½ cup of olive oil

3 lemons

½ teaspoon of salt (or exclude to reduce sodium)

½ teaspoon of black pepper

STEPS FOR COOKING

1. Wash and drain the bulgur, then place it in a large bowl. Pour ½ cup of boiling water on top of the bulgur, cover, and set aside for 30 minutes

2. Dice the tomato, chop the peeled cucumber, parsley, green onions, and mint

3. Add the vegetables to the bulgur, stirring properly

4. Extract the lemon juice and add alongside the olive oil, salt, and pepper to the bulgur mixture.

5. Before serving, set the salad at room temperature for 1 hour so that the lemon juice and olive oil is absorbed.